BIRDS FOR KIDS

Budgerigar, page 54

BIRDS
FOR KIDS

A JUNIOR SCIENTIST'S GUIDE
to Owls, Eagles, Penguins,
and Other Bird Species

MELISSA MAYNTZ

callisto publishing
an imprint of Sourcebooks

Images by iStock/Getty Images: © Mitchell Torjman: front cover; © insemar: 8; © gnagel: 15; © Dennis Sihaloho: 20; © eugenesergeev: 63 Shutterstock: © KarepaStock: ii; © Paul Reeves Photography: 10–11; © Charles Marsh Photography: 26–27, 34; © Kenneth Sewards: 29, 64; © David Uthe: 30; © Corrado Pravisano: 31; © Jean Landry: 32; © Michael G. Mill: 33; © FotoRequest: 35; © Steve Byland: 36; © montree hanlue: 37; © Don Mammoser: 38; © Bonnie Taylor Barry: 39, 62; © Jemny: 40; © Julian Popov: 41; © Brian Lasenby: 42; © Paul Sparks: 43; © Brian Lasenby: 44; © Josef Stemeseder: 45; © COULANGES: 46, 60; © Aniruddha Singhamahapatra: 47; © Werner Baumgarten: 48; © J Edwards Photography: 49; © Will Zheng: 50; © Steve Byland: 51; © Shawn Hempel: 52; © Elliotte Rusty Harold: 53; © Ondrej_Novotny_92: 54; © Jeff Caverly: 55; © Jim Cumming: 56; © Harold Stiver: 57; © Harry Collins Photography: 58; © Fiona M. Donnelly: 59; © Henner Damke: 61 © Bruce Rankin: 2, 3, 5, 6, 7, 10, 11, 13, 14, 16, 17, 18, 21, 22, 23, 24, back cover Alamy: © Arterra Picture Library: vii; © All Canada Photos: viii
Author photo courtesy of Robin Curry
Series Designer: Junior Scientists Design Team
Art Director: Keirsten Geise
Art Producer: Sue Bischofberger
Editor: Maxine Marshall
Production Editor: Jael Fogle
Production Manager: Riley Hoffman

Published by Callisto Publishing LLC C/O Sourcebooks LLC
P.O. Box 4410, Naperville, Illinois 60567-4410
(630) 961-3900
callistopublishing.com

Library of Congress Cataloging-in-Publication data is on file with the publisher.

This product conforms to all applicable CPSC and CPSIA standards.

Source of Production: Versa Press
Date of Production: January 2024
Run Number: 5037702

Printed and bound in the United States of America.

VP 10 9 8 7 6 5 4 3 2 1

CONTENTS

CONTINUED →

BIRDS UP CLOSE (*CONTINUED*)

CONCLUSION 65

American Flamingo, page 61

Atlantic Puffin, page 41

WELCOME, JUNIOR SCIENTIST!

Studying birds is fascinating! A person who studies birds is called an **ornithologist**. Anyone can be an ornithologist, no matter where they live or how old they are. I have loved birds all my life, from the jays that woke me up before school, to the hummingbirds my grandmother fed, to the cardinal that visited my very first bird feeder. Now is your chance to discover the wonderful world of birds.

In the first part of this book, you'll learn about all the things that make birds special, including their nests, their babies, how they travel, and what they eat. You'll practice thinking like a scientist as you discover where and how birds live. In part 2, you'll meet thirty-five incredible birds up close, through fun photographs and exciting facts.

This book is also your guide to hands-on exploration! "Junior Scientist in Action" activities encourage you to learn more about birds in fun ways, like by measuring your **wingspan** or building a nest.

Are you ready to take flight and discover more about birds you see every day as well as some of the most amazing birds from all over the globe? Let's fly!

Canada Goose, page 50

PART ONE
REMARKABLE BIRDS

Birds are incredible animals. In the coming pages, you'll follow birds from baby to adult. You'll learn how birds find their homes, how they build nests, what they like to eat, and more. You'll discover amazing facts. Did you know that even though most birds fly, some birds can run faster than humans? Some birds can go months without eating. Other birds can even drink while flying. Let's spread our wings and get started!

Getting Familiar with Our Feathered Friends

Birds are found in all different types of **habitats**, from forests to deserts to mountains. They live almost everywhere. Maybe you've even seen birds in your neighborhood. But do you know what makes a bird a bird?

All birds have feathers and beaks, and they all lay eggs. They are all **vertebrates**, which means they have a backbone. Most birds have wings, but not all birds fly. About sixty bird **species** around the world can't fly. This includes penguins, ostriches, emus, cassowaries, and the kakapo (*Strigops habroptila*), a parrot in New Zealand.

Bird feathers are made of **keratin**, the same stuff that makes up our hair and fingernails. A bird's longest, strongest feathers are the tips of its wings and its tail. The softest feathers are on its chest and belly.

Kakapos are parrots that can't fly!

Birds don't have teeth. Their mouth is called a beak or bill and can be very strong. The shape of a bird's beak shows what kind of food a bird eats. A triangular bill like a cardinal's or finch's is best for eating seeds. A hooked bill like that of a hawk is built for tearing apart meat. The needlelike bill of a hummingbird is for sipping sugary-sweet nectar from flowers.

Diagram of a bird

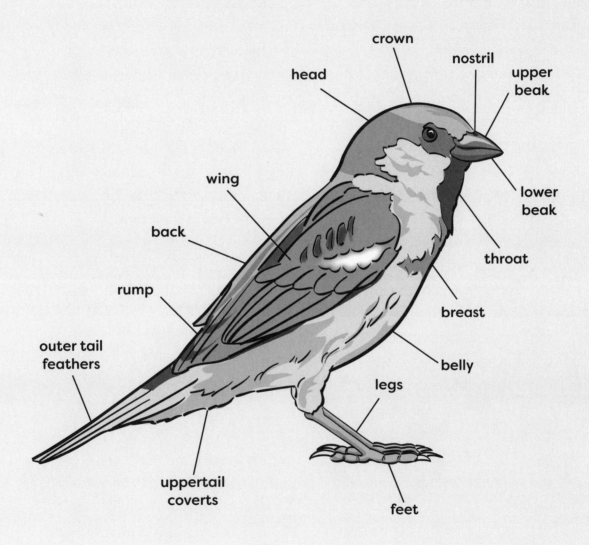

crown

head

nostril

upper beak

wing

lower beak

back

throat

rump

breast

outer tail feathers

belly

legs

uppertail coverts

feet

Different colors or markings can help you identify the birds you see. There are a few good places on a bird's body to look for markings. Notice markings on the crown or the top of a bird's head, the nape or back of its neck, or the sides of its belly. A bird's throat, chest, and tail can also be colored in ways that help us identify them.

Most birds make sounds. Some are songbirds. Robins, chickadees, and bluebirds whistle, warble, trill, and chirp pretty songs. Other birds make different sounds. Ducks quack, coo, honk, and whistle. Owls hoot, screech, and hiss.

Some birds, like woodpeckers, make noise by hitting their beaks on a tree, fence, or roof, just like a drummer. Other birds can mimic, or sound like, other things. The northern mockingbird (*Mimus polyglottos*) can make noises like cell phones, creaking doors, or car alarms.

Every bird has a scientific name and a common name. Some have more than one common name! A scientific name is a special name that scientists give a plant or animal. A bird's scientific name tells some information about what other birds it is related to. Sometimes scientific names are long and hard to read! So people give birds common names that are easier to say and remember. This book uses a bird's most popular common name and includes its scientific name the first time the bird is mentioned.

Baby Birds

All birds hatch from eggs. Since all bird species are not alike, baby birds can be very different, too.

Some baby birds, like ducks, geese, swans, turkeys, and sandpipers, are covered with soft feathers when they hatch. Their eyes are open, and they can walk and run immediately. Baby ducks and geese can even swim right away. These types of baby birds are called **precocial**.

Baby songbirds are almost bald when they hatch. Like very young puppies or kittens, their eyes are closed,

Baby ducks hatch with their eyes open and can walk right away.

and they can't move much. These baby birds are called **altricial**. They need more care from their parents. Baby woodpeckers, songbirds, and hummingbirds are altricial.

No baby birds are able to fly right away. Their wings are too small, and their feathers are not big enough. For the first two or three weeks of their lives, they need to eat a lot, just like human babies. Parent birds spend a lot of time gathering food for their offspring.

When baby birds are ready to leave the nest, they are called **fledglings**. This means they have "fledged," or left the nest. Fledglings still need their parents to protect and feed them for several days as their feathers grow, their wings get stronger, and they practice flying.

Bigger birds, like geese, swans, eagles, herons, and cranes, take longer to grow up, but they will still be ready to move out of the nest in just a few weeks' time.

Baby robins hatch with closed eyes.

SOAR HIGHER: PROTECTING BABY BIRDS

After baby birds hatch, their parents are always alert for danger. Parent birds attack **predators** like cats, snakes, and raccoons that come too close to the nest. They squawk and fly at the predators to chase them off. Other birds nearby may join in the attack to keep their nests safe, too.

Parent killdeer birds pretend to be hurt to trick predators.

Some parent birds, like the killdeer (*Charadrius vociferus*), pretend to have a broken wing to trick a predator into chasing them instead of getting near a nest. The parent bird will flop on the ground, dragging its wing like it is hurt. The hungry predator will think the hurt bird is easy to catch, but the parent bird will lead the hunter away from the nest. When the predator is far enough from the nest, the parent bird flies away!

Leaving the Nest

Birds have a lot to learn even after they leave the nest. They need to find their own homes. Some birds **migrate** every spring and fall, moving to warm areas where they can find food and have enough space to raise their families. Other birds stay in the same place year-round, changing what they eat and how they stay safe during the different seasons.

By the time most birds are a year old, they will look for a mate and begin to raise the next generation of birds. This means finding and building a safe nesting spot and guarding their own eggs and chicks. Larger birds, like eagles or gulls, may take two or three years to become full adults, even though they will still leave the nest just a few weeks after hatching.

Canadian geese learn to swim just 24 hours after hatching, and start flying around three months.

All adult birds must keep their feathers in good shape so they can fly well. Birds also must protect themselves from other dangers like pollution and bad weather.

SOAR HIGHER: FLOCKS OF FUN

There are many fun names for flocks of specific birds. How many of these have you seen?

- A flock of **hawks** is called a **kettle**, a **boil**, or a **cast**.

- A flock of **chickadees** is called a **banditry**.

- A flock of **crows** is called a **murder**, a **congress**, or a **horde**.

- A flock of **doves** is called a **bevy**, or a **flight**.

- A flock of **ducks** is called a **raft**, a **team**, or a **paddling**.

- A flock of **flamingos** is called a **flamboyance**, or a **stand**.

- A flock of **hummingbirds** is called a **glittering**, a **shimmer**, or a **tune**.

- A flock of **owls** is called a **parliament**, a **wisdom**, or a **study**.

- A flock of **penguins** is called a **colony**, a **huddle**, or a **waddle**.

- A flock of **turkeys** is called a **gobble**, a **gang**, or a **posse**.

Finding a Home

Birds live in all habitat types: deserts, woodlands, grasslands, beaches, swamps, and even in the snowy tundra of the Arctic and on the ice sheets of Antarctica.

Habitats include all the plants, water, shelter, and food sources in the natural environment. Different habitats can be very different from one another, and different birds can thrive in each one.

Downy woodpeckers live in woodland habitats.

Woodlands and jungles have the most types of birds. These habitats offer many trees for shelter. They are full of insects, small mammals, flowers, seeds, and fruits for birds to eat. Chickadees, warblers, woodpeckers, jays, and many other birds live in woodlands. Tropical parrots, hummingbirds, and sunbirds are common in jungles.

Grassland and desert habitats have fewer trees, but there are seeds, insects, and even snakes for birds to eat. Roadrunners, sparrows, vultures, and meadowlarks are common in these habitats.

Beaches and coastlines make great bird habitats. Many sandpipers, gulls, and pelicans fish along the shoreline or pick insects and worms from the sand.

Swamps and wetlands are rich habitats with a lot of slow, murky water and thick plants that are perfect spots for many warblers and wading birds like herons and egrets. Ducks are also common in these areas.

Snowy habitats might seem bare, with only rocks and a few small bushes, but plenty of birds live in the Arctic and Antarctica. Many shorebirds migrate to the Arctic for the summer, when there are plenty of insects, and some birds, like penguins, live year-round in

Ducks live in wetland habitats.

icy Antarctic habitats and hunt fish in the ocean.

Cities and towns also have many birds. Pigeons, sparrows, and hawks are right at home among tall buildings, and birds of all types can be found in parks, gardens, and yards.

HELP PROTECT BIRD HABITATS

Bird habitats are in danger from pollution, litter, trees being cut down, bug spray that kills insects, and more. Get ready to help protect bird habitats with a litter cleanup!

What You'll Need:

**TRASH BAGS
RUBBER GLOVES OR
WORK GLOVES
NOTEBOOK
PEN OR PENCIL**

1. Choose a park, beach, nature trail, or other place for your litter cleanup. Ask an adult for help finding the best place to clean up a bird habitat. Never leave home without an adult!

2. Bring trash bags, gloves to protect your hands, a notebook, and something to write with. At the park, spend one or two hours picking up litter. Be careful to avoid touching anything sharp!

3. Put garbage in one bag and items to recycle, like soda cans or water bottles, in another bag.

4. In your notebook, write down the types of litter you find. Which litter is the most common? After your cleanup, think about how the litter you found might hurt birds. What can you do to make sure there is less litter in birds' habitats?

Bird Journeys

Although about half of all birds stay in the same habitat and area all year, many birds travel. It can be a dangerous journey when birds migrate between summer and winter habitats.

Jays, owls, chickadees, quail, nuthatches, crows, finches, pigeons, and cardinals are just some of the birds that stay in the same **range**, the area they live, all year long. These birds are good at finding shelter when it is cold and can eat different foods in different seasons.

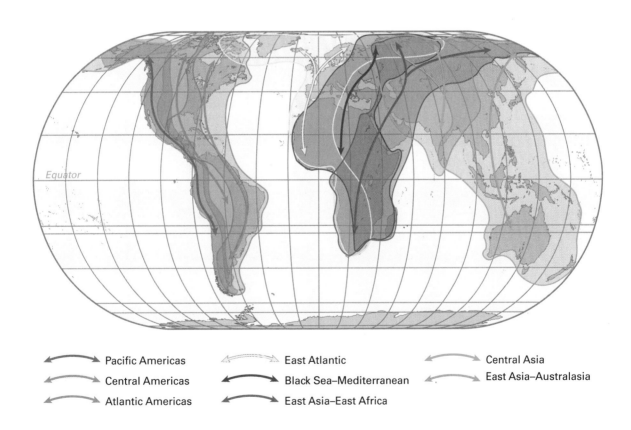

Pacific Americas

Central Americas

Atlantic Americas

East Atlantic

Black Sea–Mediterranean

East Asia–East Africa

Central Asia

East Asia–Australasia

Many other birds migrate between ranges. Hummingbirds, orioles, sparrows, warblers, hawks, ducks, and sandpipers travel hundreds or even thousands of miles every spring and fall to find the best places to live in different seasons.

When birds migrate, they must find food along the way. Some birds, like warblers, eat a lot just before they start traveling. The extra fat they gain gives them the energy they need to fly for hours every day. Other birds, like hawks, coast on the wind to make flying easier, just like airplanes use air currents to help save gas.

Bird migration is busiest in spring and fall, but birds are migrating every day of the year. Birds that travel far start migrating early because their journey takes a long time. The Arctic

Many birds migrate to follow warm weather and food sources.

tern (*Sterna paradisaea*) has the longest migration of any bird. It travels 45,000 miles from the Arctic to the Antarctic and back every year. This is the same as going from New York to California eighteen times!

SOAR HIGHER: DO BIRDS GET LOST?

When birds travel long distances, they use many different tools to **navigate**, or find their way. Some birds remember landmarks like mountains or coastlines as they travel, and they can find those landmarks each time they make the trip.

Some birds, such as sandhill cranes (*Grus canadensis*), learn where to go from their parents when they travel in family groups.

The stars even guide some birds. They can use the brightest stars to know which direction to fly.

Whooping cranes (above) migrate 2,500 miles each year.

Even with all these tools, sometimes birds get lost and might end up far from where they should be. They often find food and other birds to stay with. Lost birds can be confused until they figure out how to get where they're headed or return to where they came from.

Building a Nest

In spring and summer, birds build nests where they will lay their eggs. After the eggs hatch, bird parents raise their chicks in the nest. A nest protects the eggs and gives chicks a safe home while they grow.

Cup nests are made from sticks and are found in trees. Robins, cardinals, hummingbirds, and many other birds build cup nests. Cup nests are probably what you imagine when you think of a bird's nest, but there are many other kinds of nests, too!

Scrape nests are simple nests scraped into the ground, just like you would scrape a dent in the earth with your feet. These nests are popular on beaches or in tundra habitats where there aren't many trees. Instead of

Cup nest

Scrape nest

twigs, these birds use pebbles or grass to build their nests. Shorebirds and penguins are two kinds of birds that build scrape nests.

Burrows are nests dug deep into the ground or in a sandy riverbank. Puffins and kingfishers dig burrows, and so does the burrowing owl (*Athene cunicularia*), which lives in deserts in the western United States.

Cavity nest

Burrow

Cavity nests are built in holes inside trees or poles. Birds might bring some sticks, leaves, or grass into the hole as a cushion. Woodpeckers, chickadees, bluebirds, wrens, and parrots are all cavity-nesting birds.

Platform nest

Pendant nests are very tightly woven and hang like bags underneath branches. Orioles weave grasses together to make these bags, leaving a hole near the top so they can go in and out.

Pendant nest

Platform nests are big. They are made with big sticks and are usually flat. These nests might be reused for many years because the sticks are so strong. Eagles, herons, and egrets build platform nests.

BE A CUP NEST ARCHITECT!

Birds can take one or two weeks to build cup nests. They weave grass, twigs, straw, leaves, moss, feathers, and spiderwebs to create a cup to protect their eggs. The nest must be strong enough to be safe, but also flexible enough to hold baby birds as they get bigger and move around.

It is your turn to try building a strong nest!

What You'll Need:

BUCKET OR BASKET TO COLLECT NESTING MATERIALS
NESTING MATERIALS
NEWSPAPERS
TOY EGGS, OR SMALL ROCKS OR BALLS THAT CAN BE PRETEND EGGS

1. Explore outside to find nesting materials like small twigs, grass clippings, leaves, pebbles, or bits of bark. Put them in your bucket. Only collect materials from the ground. Do not pick live plants.

2. Lay out newspapers to protect the area where you will build your nest. This could be on a table or counter, or you can build your nest on the ground.

3. Begin by weaving materials together to make a strong "nest floor." Use bigger, stronger materials for the nest floor, and make sure it is woven tightly and doesn't have any holes the eggs might fall through.

continued

BE A CUP NEST ARCHITECT! *continued*

4. Start building up the sides of your nest by adding materials all around the edges of the floor, stacking and weaving different materials together so they will stand up.

Most nests are small, but some are huge. Bald eagle nests are as big as a car!

5. Keep working until your nest has walls and a cuplike middle. Weave materials in and out to make it stronger.

6. Put your "eggs" in the nest. Do they fit? Can you lift the nest, or do the eggs fall out?

It's okay if your nest isn't perfect. Birds are the expert architects!

Staying Clean

Birds preen to keep their feathers clean and healthy.

Just like you take baths and wash your hands, birds also need to keep clean. This helps them stay healthy and keeps their feathers in top shape so they can fly.

Some birds take baths, splashing in shallow dishes of water or puddles to get wet. Other birds use dust, rolling in very dry, fine dirt the same way other birds splash in water. The dust gets on their skin, soaking up oil. Roadrunners, quail, and sparrows all enjoy dust baths.

After a bath, birds **preen**, using their beaks and toes to wipe their feathers and remove dirt, loose feathers, or insects. They carefully stroke each feather, making sure it is in the right spot to keep them warm and allow them to fly.

Once or twice a year, birds **molt**, or shed and regrow all their feathers. Old feathers, just like old clothes, can get torn or worn out. New feathers are stronger and have brighter colors. Some birds, like the American goldfinch (*Spinus tristis*), grow different-colored feathers in different seasons. Spring feathers are much brighter and more colorful to attract a mate. Fall feathers are dull to help the bird stay hidden and safe.

SOAR HIGHER: FABULOUS FEATHERS

Birds are the only animals alive that have feathers. Millions of years ago, some dinosaurs had feathers, too!

Hummingbirds have the fewest feathers, but even these tiny birds have roughly 1,000 feathers. If you count to 10 over and over 100 times, you could count a hummingbird's feathers.

Eagles, hawks, and vultures each have about 5,000 to 8,000 feathers. This is as many as the number of Cheerios in two or three full boxes!

Larger birds, like swans, have up to 25,000 feathers. If you stacked 25,000 sheets of paper, the stack would measure almost 100 inches (or more than 8 feet) tall!

Penguins have the smallest, densest feathers, with up to 100 feathers per square inch on their bodies. This helps keep them warm and safe while they swim in icy Antarctic waters.

Some birds have extra-fancy feathers. The male Indian peafowl (*Pavo cristatus*), also known as the peacock, has very fancy feathers that grow from its lower back into a long, colorful tail. Peacocks use these feathers to show off how strong and healthy they are.

Feathers can weigh more than a bird's skeleton!

Eat Like a Bird

Birds need healthy diets so they have energy to raise families, grow strong, travel, build nests, keep clean, and stay safe. For different birds, this means different foods. Depending on the species, birds eat all types of foods, from grass and seeds to fish, fruit, bugs, and more.

Seed-eating birds are called **granivores**. They eat seeds from grasses, flowers, and even weeds. Finches and sparrows are granivores. They live in grassy habitats where there are lots of seeds.

Birds that eat fruit, including apples, oranges, cherries, and berries, are called **frugivores**. Orioles, waxwings, and grosbeaks are frugivores. Forests and woodlands are the habitats with the most fruit.

Some birds sip nectar from flowers. They are called **nectivores**. Nectar gives birds like hummingbirds and

Birds that eat fruit are called frugivores.

sunbirds lots of energy. Orioles and warblers will also sip nectar sometimes.

Birds that eat all types of plant material, including seeds, fruit, leaves, and buds, but don't eat any meat are called **herbivores**. This diet is similar to other herbivores you know, like cows and horses. Many geese and parrots are herbivores.

Many birds eat bugs, including ants, grasshoppers, gnats, mosquitoes, and even spiders and dragonflies. Flycatchers, swallows, and warblers are some **insectivores**.

Birds near water often hunt fish. When a bird eats mostly or only fish, it is a **piscivore**. Pelicans, terns, and penguins are piscivores.

Some birds hunt and eat snakes! These birds are **ophiophagous**. Herons and egrets eat snakes, and the snake eagles of Asia and Africa are snake-hunting experts.

There are also birds that hunt mollusks, like clams, oysters, and snails. Many shorebirds eat mollusks, and they are called **molluscivores**. The snail kite (*Rostrhamus sociabilis*), found in Florida and South America, is a molluscivore.

Birds that eat only meat, including mammals, amphibians, insects, fish, mollusks, or even other birds or eggs, are called **carnivores**. These birds have strong claws and sharp beaks

Birds that eat clams, oysters, and snails are called molluscivores.

to kill and tear up their prey. Eagles, hawks, falcons, and owls are carnivores.

Finally, many birds eat nearly anything, and they have both plants and animals in their diet. They may change their diet as the seasons change and different foods become easier to find or catch. These birds are called **omnivores**.

GROW FOOD FOR BIRDS

When it's late spring or early summer, get planting to feed the birds!

What You'll Need:

SPOON
SUNFLOWER SEEDS FROM BIRDSEED
PLANT MARKERS
WATERING CAN

1. Choose a warm, sunny spot.

2. Dig a small hole 2 inches deep for each seed.

3. Plant the seeds 8 to 10 inches apart, and use a plant marker to show where each seed is planted.

4. Give the seeds just a ½ cup of water every day until they sprout and show two to four leaves. After that, give the small plants 1 cup of water per day until they are 1 foot tall. Add an extra cup of water for each foot the plant grows.

5. Flowers will sprout and open after several weeks. It will take a couple more weeks for seeds to ripen. Keep watering the flowers as they ripen.

6. When the plant's leaves are dry and brown, cut off the sunflower head (ask an adult for help!). Place it on the ground for birds to enjoy.

Wild Turkey, page 34

PART TWO

BIRDS UP CLOSE

Are you ready to meet some feathery friends? It's time to get to know thirty-five wild bird species!

Each bird profile shows the colors, sounds, and behaviors unique to that bird. When you see a bird outside, compare it to the bird profiles in this book to see if you can identify its species. You may already have seen some of these birds either in your neighborhood or at a zoo. Others might be completely new to you. Let's get birding!

GO BIRDING!

Birds are everywhere! Which ones will you find?

What You'll Need:

BINOCULARS (OPTIONAL)
NOTEBOOK
PEN OR PENCIL

1. With a grown-up for company, take a walk around your neighborhood to find birds. Be sure to walk and speak quietly so you don't scare them.

2. Look at the colors and markings of the birds you see to identify different species.

3. Write notes in your notebook about where you see birds, what they look like, and what they are doing.

4. Check this book to see if you've spotted one of the birds profiled.

5. Take another walk on another day! Maybe visit a new spot to see if different birds are there, or visit your same spot at a different time of day. When and where do you see the most birds?

Bald Eagle

Haliaeetus leucocephalus

SAY IT! *ha-LEE-ate-us loo-coh-SEH-fuh-lus*

Bald eagles might be the most famous birds in America. They are our country's national bird! Bald eagles are almost always seen near lakes, rivers, or coasts where there are lots of fish to eat. Look for them perched in trees or on the ground.

Bald eagles were once endangered because of toxic chemicals called pesticides. Today, these eagles are found in many areas. They build huge nests and reuse the same nest year after year. The biggest bald eagle nest ever found was in Florida. It was more than nine feet wide and six feet long, and it weighed over 4,000 pounds. That's about the size and weight of a car!

FACT CHART

HABITAT: Wetlands, coasts

RANGE: North America from Alaska to Mexico

BEAK TO TAIL: 28–40 inches, or 2.3–3.3 feet

WINGSPAN: 70–90 inches, or 5.8–7.5 feet

COLOR: Chocolate-brown body, white head and tail

DIET: Fish, small mammals, ducks, geese

LIFESPAN: Up to 40 years

American Robin

Turdus migratorius

SAY IT! *TER-duss MY-gruh-TORE-eee-us*

American robins are the state bird of Connecticut, Michigan, and Wisconsin.

These songbirds are often seen on the grass at schools and parks, where they use their excellent eyes and ears to see and hear worms hiding underground. Worms aren't all these birds eat, though. They also love fruit and berries.

American robins are often thought of as spring birds, but many of them stay in the same areas all winter if they can find enough food. Add slices of apples or small berries to a bird feeder to give American robins a special treat!

FACT CHART

HABITAT: Nearly everywhere; woodlands, parks, and yards

RANGE: North America from Alaska to Mexico, Bahamas

BEAK TO TAIL: 8–11 inches

WINGSPAN: 12–16 inches

COLOR: Black head, gray body, orange-red breast, white under tail

DIET: Fruit, worms, insects

LIFESPAN: 2–3 years

Mallard

Anas platyrhynchos

SAY IT! *AH-nahs PLAHT-eee-RING-kohs*

Mallard ducks live almost everywhere. You can recognize a male mallard by his green head, gray-brown flanks (sides), yellow bill, and the tight curl on his tail. Females have brown feathers.

These ducks might be seen on nearly any pond, in swamps, rivers, or lakes, or even on golf courses or in city parks. They gather in large flocks and are comfortable sharing space with other duck species.

If you visit mallards at a local park, don't feed them bread! It is best to let ducks find their own natural foods like plants, insects, and small fish.

FACT CHART

HABITAT: Wetlands, waterways

RANGE: North America, Europe, Asia, northern Africa, Australia, New Zealand

BEAK TO TAIL: 20–25 inches

WINGSPAN: 33–37 inches

COLOR: Green head, gray body, black tail (males); mottled brown and cream (females)

DIET: Insects, plants, mollusks, seeds, small fish

LIFESPAN: 2–3 years

Killdeer

Charadrius vociferus

SAY IT! *kuh-RAY-dree-us voh-SIH-fer-us*

Killdeers like habitats with short, dry grass and gravel, which they use for their nests. Look for these birds in parking lots, golf courses, abandoned lots, and dry fields.

The killdeer is boldly marked with stripes and has bright orange around its eyes, but when these birds stand still in a dry field or patch of gravel, they can be very hard to see.

Killdeer parents are protective of their precocial chicks. Even though baby killdeers can run quickly soon after they hatch, the parents will pretend to be hurt if a predator is nearby. This fools the predator into chasing them, which keeps the babies safe.

FACT CHART

HABITAT: Grasslands, dry open spaces

RANGE: Canada to northern South America

BEAK TO TAIL: 8–11 inches

WINGSPAN: 18–19 inches

COLOR: Brown above, white belly, two black bands across the chest

DIET: Insects

LIFESPAN: 10–11 years

Black-Capped Chickadee

Poecile atricapillus

SAY IT! *POH-uh-sill AA-trih-cuh-PILL-us*

Black-capped chickadees are energetic birds that flit around trees and feeders. They are very curious and will investigate strange sounds.

These birds stay in the same area year-round. They love visiting bird feeders for sunflower seeds, suet, and peanuts. Black-capped chickadees also nest in birdhouses.

Look for black-capped chickadees in tall trees, including in parks and yards. Listen carefully, because these birds are often heard before they are seen. They sing their name with a loud "chick-a-dee-dee-dee" call.

FACT CHART

HABITAT: Woodlands

RANGE: North America from Canada to the middle of the United States

BEAK TO TAIL: 4.5–6 inches

WINGSPAN: 6–8 inches

COLOR: Gray back, white cheeks, black head and bib, pale belly

DIET: Seeds, berries, insects

LIFESPAN: 2–3 years

Wild Turkey

Meleagris gallopavo

SAY IT! *MELL-eee-ah-grihs gah-loh-PAY-voh*

The wild turkey is one of the largest birds in North America, and males have big, fanlike tails. These birds travel in noisy flocks. Their "gobble-gobble" can be heard up to a mile away!

A male wild turkey is called a tom, and a female is a hen. A younger male is a jake, and a younger female is a jenny.

Wild turkeys almost went **extinct** in the early 1900s because of hunting. Today, they can be found in forty-eight states. There are no wild turkeys in Alaska or Hawaii. Look for wild turkey flocks in grasslands, fields, and woodlands.

FACT CHART

HABITAT: Woodlands, forest edges

RANGE: United States into central Mexico

BEAK TO TAIL: 43–45 inches

WINGSPAN: 50–57 inches

COLOR: Shiny dark body, pink or pale blue head and neck

DIET: Insects, berries, nuts, seeds, grain, leaves, grass

LIFESPAN: 3–4 years

Blue Jay

Cyanocitta cristata

SAY IT! *SEYE-ANN-oh-sit-uh KRIS-tah-tuh*

Look for blue jays in parks and all over the neighborhood where there are big trees. These birds have blue and white feathers with pointed head crests. They stay in the same area all year, so you can see them in both summer and winter.

Blue jays have strong families. Male and female birds work together to build nests, care for eggs, and feed chicks. Even after young blue jays are big enough to leave the nest, the family sticks together for a few months, feeding together and playing games, like tag. Jays love nuts and bury them to save for later.

FACT CHART

HABITAT: Woodlands, parks, yards

RANGE: Southern Canada, eastern and central United States

BEAK TO TAIL: 10–12 inches

WINGSPAN: 14–17 inches

COLOR: Blue with black bars, white below, black collar and necklace

DIET: Nuts, berries, insects, seeds, grain

LIFESPAN: 4–7 years

Brown Pelican

Pelecanus occidentalis

SAY IT! *PEHL-IH-can-us OX-ih-dehnt-al-is*

The brown pelican is a large bird with a very long bill and baggy throat pouch. These birds are famous fishers! When a brown pelican fishes, it flies high above the water. When it spots fish, the bird dives headfirst into the water. It catches fish in its big bill and throat pouch.

A brown pelican's throat pouch can hold more than two gallons of water, but the bird spits out the water before swallowing the fish whole.

Look for brown pelicans flying low above the water at the beach or floating on the waves.

FACT CHART

HABITAT: Beaches, coastlines

RANGE: United States, Caribbean, Mexico, Central America, northern South America

BEAK TO TAIL: 40–54 inches

WINGSPAN: 78–80 inches

COLOR: Gray and black body, brown or white neck, white head and face, yellow-orange bill

DIET: Fish

LIFESPAN: 15–30 years

Rock Pigeon

Columba livia

SAY IT! *COH-luhm-buh LIH-vee-uh*

The rock pigeon is one of the most common birds in the world. These birds are originally from Europe and the Middle East, but today they live everywhere, especially in cities. Look for rock pigeons in any city or town, in parks and parking lots, under highway overpasses, and on city skyscrapers.

Rock pigeons are popular as pets, and they are sometimes raced as homing pigeons. During World War I and II, special rock pigeons were trained to carry messages through enemy territory!

FACT CHART

HABITAT: Cities and towns, rocky cliffs

RANGE: Everywhere!

BEAK TO TAIL: 11–14 inches

WINGSPAN: 20–26 inches

COLOR: Gray with dark bars on the wings, shiny purple or green patch on the neck

DIET: Seeds, grain, fruit, trash, crumbs

LIFESPAN: 3–5 years

Great Horned Owl

Bubo virginianus

SAY IT! *BEW-boh VIR-gihn-eee-AY-nus*

The great horned owl is a powerful raptor. It can hunt and kill animals bigger than itself, but most often it hunts smaller prey. Look for great horned owls hunting after the sun goes down, near roads or woodlands. You might see them perched on top of tall trees. Listen for their "hoo-hoo-HOO-hoo" calls, especially in January and February, when mates are singing to each other.

This owl's "horns" are not horns, or ears. They are tufts of long feathers. The owl can move its "horns" and uses them for camouflage to blend into tree trunks.

FACT CHART

HABITAT: Woodlands, swamps, farms, fields, towns, parks

RANGE: North America, Central America, South America

BEAK TO TAIL: 18–25 inches

WINGSPAN: 40–57 inches

COLOR: Brown and black with a tan face, white bib, and yellow eyes

DIET: Rodents, small mammals like rabbits, small birds

LIFESPAN: 10–15 years

Northern Cardinal

Cardinalis cardinalis

SAY IT! *CAR-dih-nahl-eees CAR-dih-nahl-eees*

The bright red northern cardinal is the state bird of Illinois, Indiana, Kentucky, North Carolina, Ohio, Virginia, and West Virginia. This bird easily comes to bird feeders, especially if you fill the feeders with sunflower seeds.

Northern cardinals stay brightly colored all year long. Male northern cardinals are red. Females are light brown, with some red on their wings, tail, and the crest on their head. Both males and females have a black mask and a bright orange beak. Young cardinals are brown like females but have a dark beak.

FACT CHART

HABITAT: Woodlands, parks, yards, fields

RANGE: Central and eastern United States and Mexico

BEAK TO TAIL: 8–9 inches

WINGSPAN: 10–12 inches

COLOR: Fire-engine red (males), light brown (females), black mask, bright orange bill

DIET: Seeds, fruit, insects

LIFESPAN: 3–4 years

Greater Roadrunner

Geococcyx californianus

SAY IT! *GEE-OH-kok-sus CAL-ih-FORE-nee-an-us*

With its strong legs and a long tail to help it steer, the greater roadrunner can run as fast as 25 miles per hour. That's faster than most people can bike!

These birds are in the mythology of many Native American and Mexican cultures. Roadrunners are said to be guardians or bring good luck. The bird's X-shaped footprints, with two toes pointing forward and two toes pointing backward, disguise which way the bird is traveling so they can't be followed.

Look for greater roadrunners along roadways and paths in dry desert habitats. They often perch on rocks to see farther and watch for prey.

FACT CHART

HABITAT: Deserts, canyons

RANGE: Southwestern United States, Mexico

BEAK TO TAIL: 20–21 inches

WINGSPAN: 19–20 inches

COLOR: Streaked black, brown, and cream with a lighter belly

DIET: Insects, lizards, reptiles

LIFESPAN: 7–8 years

Atlantic Puffin

Fratercula arctica

SAY IT! *FRAA-terr-COOL-uh ARK-tick-uh*

The Atlantic puffin is also called a sea parrot or sea clown because of its big beak with orange, yellow, white, and black stripes. The bill is only colorful in spring and summer, however. It turns black and dull orange in the winter.

Puffins hunt small fish, and they have spikes and spines on their tongues and in their mouths that help them hold fish. They can hold seven or eight fish in their bill at once.

In the wild, Atlantic puffins can be hard to see. They stay out in the ocean or on rocky islands off the coast. These birds are popular in zoos and aquariums, where you can look at them up close and learn more about them.

FACT CHART

HABITAT: Rocky coastlines, sea cliffs

RANGE: Eastern U.S. coast from New Jersey to Canada, Greenland, Europe

BEAK TO TAIL: 10–11 inches

WINGSPAN: 20–21 inches

COLOR: Black above, white below, orange legs and feet

DIET: Fish

LIFESPAN: 20–30 years

American Goldfinch

Spinus tristis

SAY IT! *SPY-nuss TRIHS-tuss*

The American goldfinch is bright yellow. Or is it? Males are yellow only in spring and summer. In fall and winter, these birds change to dull yellow-gray for better camouflage. Females are always dull colors so they stay protected when they are nesting.

The American goldfinch is the state bird of New Jersey, Iowa, and Washington.

These birds visit bird feeders and love small seeds. American goldfinches eat seeds from many different flowers, including dandelions. Look for these birds in overgrown fields where there are plenty of flowers or weeds.

FACT CHART

HABITAT: Weedy grasslands, parks, yards

RANGE: Southern Canada and the United States

BEAK TO TAIL: 4–5 inches

WINGSPAN: 7.5–8.5 inches

COLOR: Yellow and black (males); tan body, black and white wings, yellow face (females)

DIET: Seeds

LIFESPAN: 3–6 years

Northern Mockingbird

Mimus polyglottos

SAY IT! *ME-muss PAH-lee-GLAH-toes*

A northern mockingbird may learn more than 200 different songs in its lifetime. These birds are excellent mimics, which means they can sound like other birds. They can also sound like car alarms or cell phones! These birds sing all day long and into the night.

The northern mockingbird is the state bird of Arkansas, Florida, Mississippi, Tennessee, and Texas.

Look for these birds in trees or hopping on the ground hunting insects. Mockingbirds flick their wings to scare insects, making them easier to catch.

FACT CHART

HABITAT: Open grassy areas, parks, yards

RANGE: United States, Caribbean, Mexico

BEAK TO TAIL: 8–10 inches

WINGSPAN: 12–14 inches

COLOR: Gray with white underneath, black wings and tail, white wing patch

DIET: Insects, fruit, small lizards

LIFESPAN: 7–8 years

White-Breasted Nuthatch

Sitta carolinensis

SAY IT! *SIHT-uh CARE-oh-LIH-nen-sis*

The white-breasted nuthatch climbs headfirst down tree trunks looking for insects. This helps the bird find bugs in more places than if it only climbed up trees.

White-breasted nuthatches also eat seeds, which they stick into tree bark and hit with their bills to crack. This gives the birds their name "nuthatch" because they "hatch" the nut when they break the shell.

Look for these birds on large trees. White-breasted nuthatches stay in the same area all year, and they like feeders filled with sunflower seeds or peanuts, two of their favorite foods.

FACT CHART

HABITAT: Woodlands, parks, yards

RANGE: Southern Canada, United States, western Mexico

BEAK TO TAIL: 5–6 inches

WINGSPAN: 8–10 inches

COLOR: Gray above, black cap and back of neck, white face, white belly, rust red near the legs

DIET: Insects, seeds, nuts

LIFESPAN: 2–3 years

Red-Tailed Hawk

Buteo jamaicensis

SAY IT! *BOOT-eee-oh JUH-my-SEN-sis*

The red-tailed hawk is one of the most common hawks in North America. You can identify these birds as they fly by their wing pattern with dark edges.

This hawk's loud screeching call is a favorite of movie and television directors. They sometimes use the red-tailed hawk's call even when there is a different bird on the screen.

Look for red-tailed hawks near rural roads and highways or soaring in clear skies. The birds can even be seen in suburbs and cities. At least twenty pairs of red-tailed hawks nest in New York City!

FACT CHART

HABITAT: Everywhere except thick woodlands

RANGE: North America from Alaska and Canada to the Caribbean, Mexico, and Central America

BEAK TO TAIL: 18–26 inches

WINGSPAN: 45–53 inches

COLOR: Brown above, white below with a spotted band on the belly, rusty red tail

DIET: Mammals, rodents, snakes, birds

LIFESPAN: 10–15 years

Common Ostrich

Struthio camelus

SAY IT! *STREW-THEYE-oh CAM-uh-luss*

The common ostrich is the world's tallest bird. It is also the world's heaviest bird. A common ostrich can weigh up to 320 pounds, which is about as heavy as two adult humans. This bird runs up to 35 miles per hour, but it cannot fly. Instead, it uses its wings to steer.

The largest bird egg ever laid was an ostrich egg that weighed over five and a half pounds! An average common ostrich egg weighs as much as twenty chicken eggs.

FACT CHART

HABITAT: Grasslands, deserts

RANGE: Deserts in north and southwest Africa

BEAK TO TAIL: 66–110 inches, or 5.5–9 feet (total height)

WINGSPAN: 70–80 inches, or 5.8–6.7 feet

COLOR: Black (male) or brown (female) body; white tail; gray neck, head, and legs

DIET: Seeds, grain, grass, fruit, plants

LIFESPAN: 30–45 years

House Sparrow

Passer domesticus

SAY IT! *PAAS-err DOH-mess-tih-cuss*

The house sparrow is also called the English sparrow, and it's originally from Europe, Asia, and parts of northern Africa. Today, these small brown birds are found almost everywhere in the world except rain forests, very tall mountains, or the driest deserts.

Sparrows love dust baths. A whole flock will bathe in the same dry patch. The birds fling the dirt and dust everywhere as they wiggle, roll, and shake.

You might see house sparrows right in your yard, at a local park, at school, or even at the grocery store or library.

FACT CHART

HABITAT: Almost everywhere

RANGE: Worldwide except for very bare, dry habitats or very wet climates

BEAK TO TAIL: 6–7 inches

WINGSPAN: 7.5–10 inches

COLOR: Streaked brown and black, gray belly, gray cap and black bib (males), creamy eyebrow (females)

DIET: Grains, seeds, insects

LIFESPAN: 3–5 years

Barn Swallow

Hirundo rustica

SAY IT! *HIH-run-doh RUH-stik-uh*

The barn swallow uses its long forked tail and pointed wings to steer gracefully in curves, swirls, and turns. These birds need to be fast to catch bugs in the air to eat. They even drink while flying, swooping low over lakes or ponds to scoop up water in their bills.

Barn swallows build cup-shaped nests out of bits of mud, carrying mouthfuls of mud and adding glob after glob to construct their home. You can find their nests under the eaves of barns, sheds, stables, bridges, or houses.

Look for barn swallows near open, grassy areas like sports fields and golf courses.

FACT CHART

HABITAT: Open grasslands, agricultural fields, sports fields

RANGE: North America, Europe, Asia, South America, Middle East, Africa

BEAK TO TAIL: 6–7.5 inches

WINGSPAN: 11–13 inches

COLOR: Shiny dark blue above, tan below, rusty red throat

DIET: Insects

LIFESPAN: 3–8 years

Downy Woodpecker

Dryobates pubescens

SAY IT! *DREYE-oh-bayts PEW-BEE-sehns*

The downy woodpecker is common in backyards and parks. These tiny woodpeckers climb up trees and are even small enough to climb sunflowers or large weeds!

Downy woodpeckers flock with other birds like chickadees and nuthatches, especially in winter. They come to feeders where suet, peanut butter, and peanuts are offered for tasty snacks. They also love sunflower seeds.

Look for downy woodpeckers in parks and yards where there are some trees or small streams.

FACT CHART

HABITAT: Open woodlands with trees that lose their leaves

RANGE: North America from central Canada and Alaska through the 48 lower United States

BEAK TO TAIL: 5.5–6.5 inches

WINGSPAN: 10–12 inches

COLOR: Black and white above, white below, red patch on the back of the head (males)

DIET: Insects, seeds

LIFESPAN: 3–5 years

Canada Goose

Branta canadensis

SAY IT! *BRAAN-tuh CAN-uh-DEN-sihs*

The Canada goose is native to Canada and the United States. These birds are found all over the United States, even in Alaska and Hawaii, and are now in Europe and New Zealand, too! The farther north a Canada goose lives, the smaller it is, which helps it stay warm in winter.

Parent geese protect their chicks by running at an intruder, hissing, beating their wings, or biting. If you see a Canada goose family, keep a safe distance away and do not disturb the birds.

FACT CHART

HABITAT: Grasslands, marshes, farm fields, parks

RANGE: North America from Alaska and Canada to Mexico, western Europe, New Zealand

BEAK TO TAIL: 30–44 inches

WINGSPAN: 50–67 inches

COLOR: Brown body, black tail, white belly, black neck and head with white chin and cheeks

DIET: Grass, plants, berries, seeds

LIFESPAN: 15–20 years

Yellow Warbler

Setophaga petechia

SAY IT! *SEH-TOH-fay-guh PEACH-eee-uh*

The male yellow warbler is a sunny yellow bird with a few rusty streaks on its chest. Females are not as bright and do not have the streaks. All yellow warblers have big dark eyes that give them a cute and curious face.

Yellow warblers are some of the easiest warblers to see, not only because of their bright color, but also because they are widespread in forest habitats and along streams. They are even found in city parks. Watch for these birds higher up in trees, where they flit around looking for insects.

FACT CHART

HABITAT: Thicker forests along streams, wetlands, marshes

RANGE: North America from Alaska to Mexico, Central America, Caribbean, northern South America

BEAK TO TAIL: 5 inches

WINGSPAN: 6–8 inches

COLOR: Yellow, black eyes, red streaks on chest

DIET: Insects

LIFESPAN: 6–8 years

Great Blue Heron

Ardea herodias

SAY IT! *ARR-dee-uh HAIR-oh-deee-us*

The great blue heron is a tall, elegant bird that can be seen in cities and towns at ponds and near rivers. They are fun to watch as they hunt. These birds stay very quiet and still for a long time before suddenly striking for a fish, a snake, a frog, or even a baby alligator!

Although these herons can be more than four feet tall, they only weigh four or five pounds. That's the same as a two-liter bottle of soda.

FACT CHART

HABITAT: Wetlands, rivers, coasts, fields

RANGE: North America, Central America, Caribbean, northern South America

BEAK TO TAIL: 38–54 inches, or 3–4.5 feet (total height)

WINGSPAN: 66–80 inches, or 5.5–6.7 feet

COLOR: Gray body, black-and-white head, yellow-orange bill

DIET: Fish, frogs, lizards, snakes, mammals, insects

LIFESPAN: 12–15 years

Ring-Billed Gull

Larus delawarensis

SAY IT! *LORE-us DEHL-uh-WAAR-ehn-sihs*

Ring-billed gulls are also called seagulls, but they aren't only found by the sea. Ring-billed gulls are happy in many areas, including cities and towns, because they eat many different foods.

These birds even take food from picnic tables and trash cans. Human food is not healthy for birds, so try not to feed gulls! Their bills are very strong and can hurt a person if they bite. They also may not be able to tell the difference between fingers and French fries!

FACT CHART

HABITAT: Cities, towns, farms, beaches, coasts, wetlands

RANGE: North America from central Canada to Mexico, Caribbean

BEAK TO TAIL: 17–21 inches

WINGSPAN: 41–46 inches

COLOR: Gray back, white belly and neck, black wings, yellow eyes, yellow beak

DIET: Fish, insects, seeds, grain, fruit, trash

LIFESPAN: 9–11 years

Budgerigar

Melopsittacus undulatus

SAY IT! *MELL-ahp-SIHT-uh-kuss UNH-due-LAY-tuss*

These small parrots, also called parakeets, are the most popular pet birds in the world. Pet birds can be different colors like white, yellow, or light blue, but wild budgerigars are always green with a yellow face.

These birds are wild in Australia, where huge flocks of "budgies" fly around grasslands looking for seeds and fresh water. In other parts of the world, especially in Japan, escaped pet budgerigars can sometimes be seen and might even be surprise visitors to bird feeders.

You can sometimes see these parakeets in zoos as well, where they may be part of an **aviary**, or a special bird exhibit where the birds fly free and you can feed them.

FACT CHART

HABITAT: Grasslands, open woodlands	**COLOR:** Bright green, yellow face, black stripes on the back, blue tail
RANGE: Australia	
BEAK TO TAIL: 6–8 inches	**DIET:** Fruit, seeds, plants
WINGSPAN: 12 inches	**LIFESPAN:** 6–8 years (up to 12 years as pets!)

House Finch

Haemorhous mexicanus

SAY IT! *HEE-more-house MEHX-ih-can-us*

A little brown bird with red on its head and chest, the house finch is also called the Hollywood finch because they used to live only in the western United States. House finches were introduced to the eastern United States about 100 years ago, and they have spread to most of the country, except the very middle where there are only grasslands.

These birds visit feeders or gardens that grow sunflower seeds. They travel in flocks with as many as fifty birds at once, so make sure you have a big feeder!

FACT CHART

HABITAT: Cities and towns, farms, agricultural fields

RANGE: Southern Canada to Mexico

BEAK TO TAIL: 5–5.5 inches

WINGSPAN: 8–10 inches

COLOR: Streaky brown and white, red on the head, face, and chest (no red on females)

DIET: Seeds, grain, fruit, berries, nectar

LIFESPAN: 9–11 years

Wood Duck

Aix sponsa

SAY IT! *EYEKS SPAHN-saa*

The male wood duck has bright colors and bold markings that can make it look like a painted toy. Females are duller so they can stay hidden when they are sitting on a nest. Both males and females have a crest on their heads, which they move up and down to show how they feel.

These ducks live in woodlands and wetlands and nest inside hollow trees. Ducklings jump down from the nest just a few hours after they hatch. Sometimes this jump is from more than twenty feet off the ground!

Look for wood ducks in the same flocks as mallards.

FACT CHART

HABITAT: Woodlands, swamps, wetlands, cities, towns

RANGE: Canada and the United States, but not in dry deserts or very tall mountains

BEAK TO TAIL: 18–21 inches

WINGSPAN: 26–29 inches

COLOR: Brown, tan, black, white, shiny green on the head (males), red eyes

DIET: Seeds, insects, nuts, fruit, plants

LIFESPAN: 3–5 years

Turkey Vulture

Cathartes aura

SAY IT! *KUH-tharts ORE-uh*

Vultures are nature's cleanup crew, eating dead animals. A vulture's head is bald, lacking feathers. This prevents the bird from picking up germs when it reaches into a rotting dead animal for another bite!

The turkey vulture is the most common vulture in North and South America. You can identify turkey vultures by the way they hold their wings in a V shape and wobble as they fly.

When turkey vultures find something to eat, a lot of vultures gather to share the meal.

FACT CHART

HABITAT: Farm fields, grasslands, woodlands, towns

RANGE: From southern Canada through all of South America, Caribbean

BEAK TO TAIL: 25–32 inches

WINGSPAN: 67–70 inches

COLOR: Brown-black body, bald red head, white beak, white on wings and tail

DIET: Dead animals, trash

LIFESPAN: 15–20 years

Belted Kingfisher

Megaceryle alcyon

SAY IT! *MEHG-eee-SUH-real AAL-see-uhn*

The belted kingfisher is a champion fish catcher. It flies above rivers or ponds to spot a fish before diving down headfirst and grabbing the fish in its bill.

Both male and female belted kingfishers have a colorful "belt" across their white bellies. The male has a gray-blue belt that matches his back. The female is larger than the male. She has both a gray-blue belt and a rusty red belt.

FACT CHART

HABITAT: Woodlands with rivers, lakes, and ponds

RANGE: Alaska, Canada, Mexico, Caribbean, Central America, northern South America

BEAK TO TAIL: 11–14 inches

WINGSPAN: 19–23 inches

COLOR: Gray-blue above, white belly with a blue band, rusty red "belt" (females)

DIET: Fish, insects, frogs, crayfish, reptiles

LIFESPAN: 10–15 years

Ruby-Throated Hummingbird

Archilochus colubris

SAY IT! *ARK-ill-OH-kuss COH-lih-bree*

Named for the male's glittering red throat, the ruby-throated hummingbird is the only hummingbird regularly seen in most of the central and eastern United States. These tiny birds can be easy to miss, so watch closely to see them zipping by!

All hummingbirds are fantastic fliers. The ruby-throated hummingbird beats its wings more than fifty times per second. These birds can fly forward and backward, hover, fly straight up, and dive straight down.

These birds love red and pink flowers that produce nectar, which they sip with their needlelike beaks. You can also put out a hummingbird feeder to give these birds an easy sip.

FACT CHART

HABITAT: Woodlands, orchards, flowering fields, parks, gardens, yards

RANGE: Southern Canada, eastern and central United States, Mexico, Caribbean, Central America

BEAK TO TAIL: 3–3.5 inches

WINGSPAN: 3–4 inches

COLOR: Green back, head, and sides, white belly, red throat (males)

DIET: Nectar, insects, spiders

LIFESPAN: 5–9 years

Emperor Penguin

Aptenodytes forsteri

SAY IT! *app-TEN-oh-dyets FORE-stir-eee*

Emperor penguins live in Antarctica. It is possible, however, to see this largest of all penguin species in zoos and aquariums.

To survive in Antarctica, where it can get as cold as 75 degrees below zero, these penguins have thick layers of fat and very tiny, tightly packed feathers. They also huddle together to share body heat and keep each other warm.

Emperor penguins only lay one egg at a time. While waiting for their egg to hatch, they do not eat. They can go as long as two months without food. Males and females take turns traveling long distances to fish so they can feed their chicks.

FACT CHART

HABITAT: Ice shelves, ocean

RANGE: Antarctic coast and nearby ocean

BEAK TO TAIL: 39–45 inches

WINGSPAN: 30–35 inches

COLOR: Black above, black head, white below, yellow around neck

DIET: Fish, squid

LIFESPAN: 15–20 years

American Flamingo

Phoenicopterus ruber

SAY IT! *FEE-noh-CAHP-terr-us ROO-brrr*

The American flamingo is a beautiful bright pink bird with long, thin legs and a long, thin neck. While most flamingos are found in tropical areas, the American flamingo lives in parts of Florida and is sometimes spotted along coastlines anywhere from Texas to North Carolina.

American flamingos are born gray. As they get older, the small pink shrimp they eat turns them pink! An American flamingo has a big, crooked bill, and it can hold its head upside down near the water or even underwater to catch fish and insects.

FACT CHART

HABITAT: Wetlands, coastlines, lagoons, lakes

RANGE: Southeastern coast of the United States, Caribbean, northern coast of South America

BEAK TO TAIL: 45–55 inches, or 3.75–4.6 feet (total height)

WINGSPAN: 50 inches, or 4.2 feet

COLOR: Red-pink, pink legs, black on the beak

DIET: Shrimp, worms, insects, fish, seeds, plants

LIFESPAN: 40–60 years

Painted Bunting

Passerina ciris

SAY IT! *PAAS-err-EEE-nuh SEE-rees*

Male painted buntings have blue heads, green backs, and red bellies. Females are a solid lemon-lime color. Their bright colors fit right in with the thick leaves and dense brush where they live.

Because of their beautiful colors and musical songs, painted buntings were once sold as pets. This is against the law today.

Painted buntings visit feeders for small seeds and sunflower seeds. Watch for them in pairs with both males and females visiting together. They can be shy, so keep a sharp lookout!

FACT CHART

HABITAT: Wetlands, woodland edges, near streams

RANGE: Southeastern United States, Caribbean, Mexico, Central America

BEAK TO TAIL: 4.5–5.5 inches

WINGSPAN: 8.5–9 inches

COLOR: Blue head, green back, red belly and tail (males); bright lime green (females)

DIET: Seeds, insects

LIFESPAN: 10 years

Indian Peafowl

Pavo cristatus

SAY IT! *PAY-voh KRIS-taat-us*

The Indian peafowl is commonly referred to as the peacock. In fact, peacock is the name for a male peafowl, whereas peahen is the name for a female. These birds live in the wild in India, where they are celebrated as that country's national bird.

A male peafowl has a very large train, which is made up of long, flashy feathers that grow from the bird's upper back. A peafowl uses its tail, located under the train, to raise and lower the "fan" of feathers. This motion is intended to either impress females or scare off other males.

FACT CHART

HABITAT: Woodlands, agricultural fields, towns

RANGE: India; introduced in Australia, New Zealand, Florida, Hawaii

BEAK TO TAIL: 40–45 inches, or 3–4 feet (up to 90 inches, or 7.5 feet, including the train!)

WINGSPAN: 55–62 inches, or 4.6–5.2 feet

COLOR: Shiny green and blue, gray back, brown wings, brown and white body (females)

DIET: Berries, grains, snakes, lizards

LIFESPAN: 15–20 years

Bald Eagle, page 29

CONCLUSION

Congratulations, Junior Scientist, you're now a Junior Ornithologist! I hope you've enjoyed learning about both familiar birds and birds from all around the globe. There are around 10,000 bird species in the world, so there is always more to discover about our feathered friends.

Now is the time to put what you've learned to good use! With your new understanding of how birds live and what they need, you can keep the birds in your neighborhood healthy and happy. In an outside area near your home, like a yard or porch, you might hang a bird feeder and see what birds start to visit. Ask an adult for help and permission. You can also plant flowers to attract birds or add a birdbath to give visitors something to drink. As you see and study different birds, you will continue to learn what makes each one unique.

Litter and pollution can be dangerous for birds. To help birds and other animals, follow the three Rs: **R**educe, **R**euse, **R**ecycle. Pick up litter when you are outside, and volunteer to help with beach, park, or neighborhood cleanups. Try not to use chemicals like pesticides or soaps outside, and keep cats indoors to protect birds from furry hunters.

Because birds are all around us, we can take big and small actions every day to help the birds we see. Share your love of birds with your friends, classmates, and family members. Get everyone just as excited about birds as you are!

GLOSSARY

ALTRICIAL: A type of baby bird that is born without feathers and needs a lot of care from its parents; cardinals, sparrows, and hummingbirds are altricial

AVIARY: A special zoo exhibit of only birds, where birds can fly free in a very large cage, which is sometimes as big as a house

CARNIVORE: A bird that eats only meat, including rodents, mammals, reptiles, insects, fish, or even other birds or eggs

EXTINCT: When there are no members of a species left in the world

FLEDGLING: A young bird that has moved out of the nest but still needs its parents for feeding and protection; these birds are growing quickly, and they have smaller feathers than they will when they are fully mature, so they cannot fly well yet

FRUGIVORE: A bird that eats mostly fruit and berries, such as raspberries, oranges, or bananas

GRANIVORE: A bird that eats mostly grain or seeds, such as sunflower seeds, wheat, or seeds from weeds

HABITAT: The natural environment of an animal that includes food, water, and shelter

HERBIVORE: A bird that eats mostly plants, including flowers, buds, leaves, and seeds

INSECTIVORE: A bird that eats mostly insects, including spiders, beetles, gnats, flies, and wasps

KERATIN: A protein that makes up bird feathers and claws; human fingernails and hair are also made of keratin

MIGRATE: To move to different areas in spring and fall to find better food sources and/or safer places to live

MOLLUSCIVORE: A bird that eats mostly mollusks like snails, clams, and oysters

MOLT: To shed old feathers and grow new ones, most birds molt one or two times a year

NAVIGATE: To find your way from one place to another, like a bird does when flying

NECTIVORE: A bird that eats mostly nectar, a sugary-sweet liquid birds sip from flowers

OMNIVORE: A bird that eats just about any plants or animals; most humans are also omnivores

OPHIOPHAGOUS: An animal with a diet of mostly snakes

ORNITHOLOGIST: A scientist who studies birds

PISCIVORE: A bird that eats mostly fish; bald eagles, pelicans, and penguins are piscivores

PRECOCIAL: A type of baby bird born with feathers that can run or swim very soon after it hatches; ducks, geese, and chickens are precocial

PREDATOR: An animal that hunts other animals to eat

PREEN: To clean feathers using a beak or feet and toes

RANGE: The area where a bird lives

SPECIES: A group of living beings that have many things in common and can mate to make others of their kind

VERTEBRATE: Any animal that has a backbone

WINGSPAN: The length of a bird's wings from wingtip to wingtip

INDEX

Acknowledgments

It took the effort of a whole flock of birds to write this book. Many thanks to Lana, Julia, and Maxine for reaching out to me and seeing potential in the project, and for guiding it on every page to be its very best. To all the unnamed others on the Callisto Publishing team who worked with edits, layouts, photos, images, resources, and so many other aspects of helping this book take flight, my never-ending thanks.

To all the birds I've enjoyed throughout my life, and every bird I have yet to see, thank you for your fun and feathery inspiration.

To all the readers of my articles, books, and blogs, thank you, most sincerely.

For Trevor, just because.

And to my husband, Marc, who has always believed in me even when I don't. Your love and support is and always will be priceless. My thanks, my love, and my heart are always yours.

About the Author

Melissa Mayntz is an enthusiastic birder and award-winning author who has traveled to see birds all over the world, including Alaska, Hawaii, Jamaica, Italy, Mexico, Honduras, and Israel. She has written hundreds of articles about birds, and her first book, *Migration: Exploring the Remarkable Journeys of Birds*, describes how birds migrate and how we can help birds keep safe as they travel. Today, Melissa lives in Florida, where she enjoys seeing painted buntings, northern mockingbirds, and many other birds at her feeders. Visit her website at BeYourOwnBirder.com to discover more about birds and how to enjoy birding in your own unique way.